Berry's First
COLLECTION

Berry's First COLLECTION

Dream /Fantasy/ Reality

CHANGES III

Berry's First Collection
Copyright © 2019 by Changes III. All rights reserved.

No part of this publication may be reproduced, stored in a retrieval system or transmitted in any way by any means, electronic, mechanical, photocopy, recording or otherwise without the prior permission of the author except as provided by USA copyright law.

The opinions expressed by the author are not necessarily those of URLink Print and Media.

1603 Capitol Ave., Suite 310 Cheyenne, Wyoming USA 82001
1-888-980-6523 | admin@urlinkpublishing.com

URLink Print and Media is committed to excellence in the publishing industry.

Book design copyright © 2019 by URLink Print and Media. All rights reserved.

Published in the United States of America

ISBN 978-1-64367-276-2 (Paperback)
ISBN 978-1-64367-275-5 (Digital)

Poetry Inspirational
22.02.19

A Veteran's Loss

Veterans go into battle,
With the foe machine gun to vest.
Toe to toe, bringing freedom with every death,
Until there is nothing left.
Coming home seems to be a dream,
Fighting for hollow value at times, it seems,
The VA scandal is a sore spot
By leaving veterans in the hallways to rot,
All of this must stop
Cease to find veterans shelter
And increase the health and peace!
A veteran's loss

When the Sky Cries

"The sky cries" when someone dies,
Also does the sky cry when someone is telling a lie!
Your every drop is like words,
Telling me what you've heard.
So please don't be shy
Remember my friend,
This is between You and I
Tell me about you and your entire splendor"
For one day, to you my spirit I will "surrender."
You must guide me to my new home
And I always know while with you I'm never alone.
So, cry and cry hard if you must,
For in me you can surely trust.
Yes! I feel you.
I hear you.
I will always be here for you!
So cry,
the Sky

Don't Stop!

Please don't stop what you've been doing,
Your success is around the corner.
I understand it's been very hard,
But you've come so far.
Never forget who you are.
You're the best!
Now give yourself the test of weakness.
When you're at this point
Rise above your bad side,
Rise up and succeed.
And if your motive and greed are stardom,
Then shall it be!

Want to Be the Best

I want to be the best.
Come all from the east and west.
All coming to see and give me the test.
I've always told my mom,
No matter what life throws my way
I'll dig in deep for my very best.
Will I drop, or will I rise?
Won't I shock everyone with my grand surprise!
Time will be my answer,
Until the end, my best will be done
I want to be the best of the best.

The Soul of the Ocean

Sometimes, you can be so beautiful.
With your blues and greens.
Sometimes, you're so calm and other times, you're too mean!
As sometimes, I watch you from afar,
Trying to figure out what you're really are.
You're always moving forward then back.
I'm still trying to understand
That you are just waiting to attack.
Or when something goes down,
Do you have my back?
The Soul of the Ocean

My dear ocean,
I've noticed your waves are big and wild.
Is this your forever forceful style?
Please be kind to surfers and mankind alike
As well as the beach bum,
Who sleeps on your sand at night.
When I sit upon your sand and look on you
And listen to everything you say,
I look back up to the sky and ask why,
Oh why do I have to cry?
Here we are again just you and I,
Our souls mended.
Together and I don't know why?
The Soul

A Mother's Hardship

Yes, you're in for a treat;
All my life I've sensed defeat.
Mom, you weren't apparently around,
But now my feet are on solid ground.
You sense money and come around,
I've been alone emotionally for years,
there was nobody around.
To share my tears, or fears.
I been self-sufficient in my ways.
Still I sit back and count the days,
When I can look back at the past and smile,
But I'm sure this won't happen for a while.
I go back and forgive your faults,
Because this was a talent that was self-taught.
Mother Hardships

Death on Swift Wings

Death on swift wings,
What are you crying for?
Dying isn't crying;
Dying is at long last flying!
Flying around "free" as a bird.
If you've been good
You can stop when you hear Gods words.
Dying is like walking through "plush meadow"
With the wind blowing,
Like you've never felt before!
But nothing compares when Saint Michael opens that front door for you,
And you ask is this a dream?
And he replies, no this is all cream, babies!
So, enjoy yourself
And enjoy all that be well!
Because trust me…
"You sure aren't in hell.
Death on swift wings. Silence!

Losing a Father

Now that I've lost a father,
Why should I even bother?
With life that is now my life
Seem like a bad play,
Somewhere I really don't want to stay.
Just put me in the ground next to my dad,
I know that sounds pretty sad.
However, deep inside I'm so mad
About the way life left me alone
Without a father now, my plight is known
Tell me and yourself to belong?

Untitled

Once again into the darkness
In search for the light in lucid sight
To think today once more than right
To think today just once more!
Is this all life has in store for me?
Or can one be like sap
Running through a tree with a branch
Pointed back directly toward me.

Clearance of Self

This is obviously for the clearance of self
It's just me here and I see no one else,
Careful not to step on anyone's toes
With life set before me just in front of my nose.
I know the score and try to cope,
I ask for much mercy and plenty of hope.
For my objective is lucid and clear,
And I approach life without fear.

Reflection of One's Self

I notice my mind becoming wiser year by year
Onward, I continue without any core of regret or fear!
I'm always at watch
With my mind's eye looking how time flies
Owning the innate core of my own truth
Sometimes, perfect and other isn't cute
I look in the mirror and see things unaware
Going through this life without a care
I realize my flaws and wanted to share
No longer will this occur without an ear or a single
Care.

Deep in Thought

I'm sitting here deep in thought
Dreaming of a world without rot
Holding the hands of peace and unity
As clear to me as far as the eye can see
The figure in the dark certainly is me
Can I change my history and flaws?
No, I cannot without reaching for a new plot
But I'm still here in deep thought!

Time in Time Out

Marvel in the beauty of the forest
This is what this poem is mostly about
We climb, and we fall
Please allow to brief all of ya'll,
I've been here once
And listening to the sky that's mighty fun
Hurt from the flaws of a man plans to hear
And listen to trees form the desert and sand
I'm still a man time in and time out!

Don't Know What to Do

I'm sitting quietly to myself
And don't know what to do except.
To start writing and maybe just maybe, I get the clue.
I've been writing since I was twenty-three
But still, truly, is this really me?
I think poems are insightful
And many times, "oh" so delightful
But still, is all this ambiguity really real,
Please understand this is how I truly feel
Pass or come what may
This be the place I shall always stay.
Don't know what to do

Untitled

Once more into the fusion
Life halts without conclusion.
Head back tilted to the sky
A single leave fall by
Silence hovers over the calm
Be lucid and be strong
Believe, to believe....

Opportunity of Love

I choose to sample a taste of love
Soft as a touch of a silk glove
Hold me tight all through the night
Fail to cease and increase the understanding
Forgive for the times I seem too demanding
I love too hard and ever so strong at times
With my love, I apologize
Through this and seal spoken rhyme.
Opportunity and love

Family Ties

Family and blood bonds us together
Through this crazy life we are as feathers
Floating through stormy weather
Approaching separation without preparation
Jesus be with us all.
Next to you I would like to always stand tall
Be there with me until the end
True to heart, your an enduring friend
Delighted in family bliss
I seal all our farewells with a single kiss.
Family ties...

Need Another Job

I know we need another job
Each day, I feel as if I'm being robbed
Punching a clock and there goes time
Tick-tock, look who's still messing with the same old clock,
I know I need to stop
With the same
Could it be?
I wonder could it be,
A world that exist without me
Trap in the illusion of self
I'm stuck in my mind without anyone else
Wisdom is mine to seek without rest
Have I really done my very best?
I know my life has meaning
Through and through, please,
I ask what I should do
Pause, think, and rest right...?
Will my story end with this plight?
NO...

Untitled

I try because I can
I try to be a man
I try to open doors
I try to be always more
I try to be the best
I want to inspire the rest
I try forevermore
Test me!

Untitled

Grey is my life,
Ever grey and true
Eyes wide open
And only open to you
Find your place and sit-a-spell
Know that in spirit I am doing well
Valuable is the knowledge that was gained
Our main aim was to maintain,
And we did!
Now check our status...follow me kids!
Untitled

Insightful Thoughts

I bring forth a multitude of thoughts
Sitting in a chair thinking of…oh how I've fought
Standing close in a distant world,
Sharing all my splendor with my one true girl,
I go forward and back,
Yet still not really understanding that?
Insightful thoughts!

School Days

School days are here once more
Who knows the anguish that lies in store?
Test and examinations,
Is this who I really am?
I've been going since the age of three...
Will I ever finish? Please, Lord, oh let it be
Obtaining a fabulous job to call my own
While my mind is stuck in the zone,
Which zone does?
You ask the one that's finally done with class.
Never again will I enter school,
Now I've graduated and chilling with the best,
And will go home and take a rest!
School days!

Last Breath until There Is Nothing Left

How dare one says I'm behind the curve
Outside of closed curtain,
Thinking of the days passed and gone
Like us, twinkling in the sky at night
Not knowing can be quite a fright
Air in my lungs goes up and down
Strong but without a sound!
Looking toward the next life
And will it come?
I won't sit and wait
Because that make me dumb
And my life is a poetic story
Please Lord, put a crown on my head
And fill me with the glory.
Last breath!

Sometimes I'm wrong

I can see that something is wrong
Because for some reason,
They're not playing my sweet song.
I prayed and stayed true,
I sat back and watched the world
With my mind's eye wide open
With deep intent and much focus...
I have enjoyed the history that was
I've put both hands together and looked above
Wondering is this really it for me,
or is my glass filled with distain and misery?
I've done my part,
I just want a clean fresh start.

Behind the Curve

How dare one says I'm behind the curve
How can one presume to know?
And have such nerve,
Just looking for a chance
To enhance my status in my life,
Do I dare say it more than twice?
But I am now here, relax one's mind
Including fear, appreciate the knowledge
Given now, one can see I'm truly driven.
Behind the curve!

Love Clock is One and the Same

As happy as the day is long for you
Do I release this poetic and beautiful song?
You're my saving grace,
I would do anything to see your face,
No one knows how my heart breaks
Wish you could be here
Knowing I always have your ear,
You're like solid rock
And when I imagine you my heart stops,
For a moment or two makes me thankful for loving you,
Even when I'm alone,
My heart continues singing our sweet song.

Steady Love Absent but Not Forgotten

Love is in the air,
Without a single worry or care,
Know that I will be with you during times of struggle.
I take comfort in knowing that we are indeed true lovers.
Being without you is a challenge to me
Through and through but erased because you are you!
I think of you both at night and day.
Your name I take to the Lord when I always pray.
Love you dearly and sincerely,
Can't wait until the day you are near me once again,
Because after all you are my best friend.
Love, peace and more love.
If I could, I would release a dove!

A Creative Mind

I will say blessed is the creative mind
All would be thoughts so rich and divine.
Spending time alone in my head wondering
About the possibilities now this is said,
Will live my ambitions, please won't.
Someone gives an ear and listen,
I speak of truth with
A mighty voice this is my path and my choice.
A creative mind

A Poet's Dream

What are a poet's dreams,
And what do they actually mean?
Pulling out words from the heart and soul,
Releasing the flow with no control,
Being one... with the words that we choose
Going for broke with nothing to lose
Begging for the public's ear,
Climbing to the top of the ladder without any fear,
After you review this poem...
Please, give a cheer.
A poet's dream

A Rose Grows

I believe a rose grows tall
Even, when you see it coming from a wall
We stand and glance from a distance
It just takes a few moments to listen
The pain that it has encounter
The force from the world has truly mounted,
Stand hard and true for the rose
Trust me it knows, it knows
Help the rose to grow large and tall
Then, we all can have a grand ball
The rose grow

Barry's Prospective

My prospective is simply to meet all objectives,
Being outstanding in all that I do.
Meaning being excellent and staying true
Life is filled with ups and downs,
And searching for those who continuously stand around.
In search of my life's mission
And to share with those who give an ear,
This entire brief, new edition.
Everyone has a life story
Usually for money and glory,
But I just need to tell my story.
Money that's funny to me,
Because true poets would do all this for free.
I just wanted my voice heard.
Cool, you can call me a nerd, but nothing,
Absolutely nothing, will stop me from publishing this word.
My perspective.
Now I have met my objective!

Friend Lost yet Found

I started with a friend in every which way.
I sometimes think of them when I lay down to pray.
I was searching for a true friend and a home indeed;
I met falsehoods and fakers with greed.
My plight is simple and not complicated,
But to all those who came it was very much jaded.
I prayed up to Jesus for a solid solution,
To the revolution on me;
And he said be calm, my child, I won't let this be.
Your friends are evil and full of distrust,
But put your faith in me, this you must.
Friend lost yet found.

Eye within an Eye

I started with an eye,
Seeing the world with such distrust,
It makes me ponder and sometimes cry without trust.
Why must I live in such a crazy place?
Distrust is everywhere
People going about their businesses without a single care.
I work and work, which seems like a cease to no end,
Please someone tell me when will my life truly begin?

My mind's eye is looking and probing for "hope"
Will I find resolve… maybe, yes or maybe, either way I shall grow.
Not adapting to this life, but instead having it adapt to me,
This is my way now I truly can see.
One eye, two, eye shall I continue to cry?
No, never again!
For I will have risen my friend.
Eye within an eye!

Being an Artist

Being an artist is a contradiction indeed!
Everyone will say one need to go to school.
In order to cure, heed my warning
And make your own choice
Because by becoming an Artist you've got a strong voice.
So, to increase the peace to heal the pain
Once you've shared your artistic talents things will change.
So, see your future and see it clear as day
Meaningful plights could make someone's day.
So, if it's up to me an artist is the thing to be!
If you don't want to be a robot, then follow me.
The artist!

To My Oldest Sister

My eldest sister, to whom I've adored always.
Your love means more, more, and more.
Sometimes our words are misunderstood
And the love seams to fade,
Hiding and lurking inside the shade.
To rise with the sun again like a phoenix
From the aches just to remind both me and you
No matter what we do, we're sister and brother
And there's nobody like you and me.
Sister and brother love

Lies and More Lies

Telling a lie will eventually make someone cry
It could help let someone die from sadness
A lie only suits oneself and no one else
Despite what you think when someone lies
You can't blink around them
It's so hard to say yet I still pray
For years, for hours of our day, I pray
And hope they will take the right way,
It's so hard to say
But the truth and truth it's so beautiful then lies
When it stops there are no more "cries"
And no more lies!

Men among Boys

A gentleman among boys
That's who I am to see the world differently, oh boy!
Can I see to be weary of all issues that makes one's self a man
A gentleman is a higher form of life than a simple man.
A gentle man opens doors
And some much more and would not strike a lady
And does not cuss! And is not big on making a fuss
Yet he is steady and calm
Knowing God gave him the biggest gift of all class.
So not being a savage known as an animal
Like nature with this trait is to put the human race into turmoil.
I think, in order for a man to become a gentleman,
He needs much confidence in self.

To Poetry, My First Love

Poetry, my first and true love,
You're always there for me
And I appreciate that
How you've comfort me in times of need
Writing your words is like every breath
You're as strong in my eyes like air inside my chest
This I must confess you're like a summer breeze
On a hot day sort of like a blessing from Jesus when I pray
You've changed me in so many ways
In which words cannot express

Knowing all your ways brings out my very best.
I appreciate all you've done
You're like a smoking hot gun
I use you to get things done
Poetry, my first love, sent to me from the man up above
Thanks a million!

My Outlook on Life

Do not sit down and wait on fate
That within itself would be a mistake
Go get what you've always wanted
And when you get, it you can flaunt it
Some people will tell you to get an education
But sometimes that isn't it or the right situation.
So just do what you love no matter what it is
Or else your life will always be a pop quiz,
Find what you're good at.
It could be a hidden talent
So, do a little research
It won't hurt to find the truth about you
And do what you do.
Peace and love!

Sitting Awaiting My Turn

Since the day I was born,
I've sat and waited for my turn
Sometimes coming in last
"Oh" how does my spirit and heart burns.
As the day is long
So, shall it be my turn
To be a part of everyday life
Shall I be single or suit a wife?
Will I be the head?
Guy in charge or is the wool being pulled over
My eyes while I'm being robbed blind?
Sitting awaiting my turn
Do I sit and wait for my turn to come?
While not so nice people are calling me dumb?
Or should I stand up and give it everything
I've got at least I would have known I had confidence in my life's plot
Sitting awaiting my Turn
So no longer shall I sit down and wait
Because I know in heart, body, and soul
It was not my fate, so no longer,
No longer sitting and waiting for I have changed.

Stress 123

Here I go let's talk about stress
Man, this thought is never truly at rest,
I'm continuously in such for the ultimate solution
To which there is none.
Yet I want to be the best I can be
Doing good for the entire world to recognize and see
I wish more could be in my endeavors
To become recognized and published
Would be mighty clever as 1, 2, and 3
Stress events 123!

Friendship's True Meaning

Friendship isn't something that can be bought
It is a relationship that grows overtime,
Just like writing fine poetry at times
I stay because I choose to be there for you
You can be heartless and cruel with no regret
In times of trouble you begin to fret!
Times dictate a true friend with question without
Because now I got your attention now you pause?
Friendship

www.ingramcontent.com/pod-product-compliance
Lightning Source LLC
LaVergne TN
LVHW021741060526
838200LV00052B/3394